Santa Monica City Librarian Elfie Mosse (at right with parasol) and library staff celebrate Pioneer Days in 1930.

The Santa Monica Public Library

1890-1990

by
Ellen Braby and Janet Hunt

Santa Monica, California
1990

ISBN 0-87062-204-8
LIBRARY OF CONGRESS CATALOG CARD NUMBER 90-63346

Published under the direction of
The Arthur H. Clark Company
P.O. Box 14707
Spokane, WA 99214

Dedicated to all the staff
of the Santa Monica Public Library,
past and present.

Contents

Illustrations

Acknowledgments

The authors wish to acknowledge that this book would not have been possible without the help of many people. Thanks are due to Nellie "Dolly" Sullivan, Rosemary Jamieson, Virginia McShane, Jane Buell, Carol Aronoff, Thelma Hansen and Barbara Ferstead. Special thanks to Cynni Murphy for her help with the photographs and to Molly Richardson for her help with editing the manuscript.

Special thanks to the Friends of the Santa Monica Public Library for the financial support to publish this history, and for their ongoing committment to excellence in library service.

CHAPTER 1

The Main Library

In 1850 California was admitted to the Union as the 31st state, and the vast land grants of the Sepulveda, Reyes, Marquez, and Machado families were surveyed by the Board of Land Commissioners. But the era of such grants was ending, overrun by the beginnings of urban life and fueled by competition between rival railroad lines to link the west with the rest of the nation.

As the climate of Southern California began to lure vacationers to the area, Colonel Robert S. Baker, a rancher, who had become wealthy selling mining supplies during the Gold Rush years, visited the area and began purchasing land intending to establish a sheep ranch. By 1874 Baker's holdings included portions of the present area of Santa Monica, Rustic Canyon and Pacific Palisades. His vision of a rural paradise was superceded by the potential for commercial development which centered on the creation of a proposed railway line to end at a wharf near the foot of the present Colorado Avenue where steamships would dock.

Senator John P. Jones of Nevada, whose silver mining interests had made him a millionaire, came to Santa Monica with ample funds to purchase some of Baker's holdings. He also had plans for a townsite bounded by the bay on the west, 26th Street on the east, Colorado Avenue (then known as Railroad Avenue) on the south, and Montana Avenue on the north. On July 10, 1875, with the recording of the town-site map by Los Angeles County, Santa Monica was officially a town. Five days later, the first lots were sold at auction for $200 to $500.

The auctioning of lands continued and nine months later Santa Monica had 1,000 residents, 160 houses, 75 tents, a school district, a church, a water reservoir, the wharf, a bathhouse, a hotel, and the Santa Monica *Outlook* news-paper. It was in this spirit of a new community that the Santa Monica Public Library had its beginnings. A Library Association was formed in 1876; the annual $2 dues were used to purchase books. Members of the Association in-cluded the president, Dr. J.S. Elliott, Treasurer George Boehme, and Secretary M.C. Olmstead. Weekly meetings were held to discuss books and read papers. There were at least 25 members at one time but how long the organization lasted and what became of the books purchased is not recorded.

In the next few years, the area went through mixed times. Despite the hope that the town would be a popular shipping destination, the rail line was sold and the wharf closed in 1878. Many who had rushed to buy land and build were unable to make a living and left, but the location and climate attracted others, and the community slowly continued to grow.

Eight years after the Library Association was started, a new attempt to fund a free reading room was started by several prominent women, including Mrs. Asenath Larimer and Miss Ellen Dow. Their enthusiasm generated support from many, including Colonel Baker. A room adjoining Dr. Fred C. McKinnie's drug store was used as the reading room until the ladies turned it over to the newly formed Women's Christian Temperance Union in 1888. The WCTU moved the reading room to their building on Third Street. At this time, the collection of books numbered 400, plus popular magazines and newspapers. Anyone could use the material in the room free of charge, but members paid 25 cents a month for books taken from the room. In an article in July 1888, the *Evening Outlook* described this room as one of the "specially inviting places in Santa Monica" and praised the women of the WCTU for their hard work on the behalf of the readers of the city.

Supporting the reading room was a constant struggle. The ladies of the WCTU gave dinners and suppers, socials and fairs. At one dinner they catered, an auction of property on the South Side, the owner offered a commission of $100 to the ladies if they could sell the house and lot. Mrs. D.B. Hubbell found a buyer and made the sale. When she received the money, she promptly gave it to the library fund "and the day on which she spent a hundred dollars all at once for books for the Santa Monica library was a red letter day in her life," according to *Ingersoll's Century History, Santa Monica Bay Cities.*

In 1888, several ladies from Santa Monica entered an exhibit in the second Floral Festival held in Hazard's Pavilion in Los Angeles. The Santa Monica entry consisted of a full-rigged ship floating in Santa Monica Bay with the Palisades in the background, all made of flowers. The Santa Monica booth won the first prize of $200 which was turned over to the reading room after deducting expenses.

Despite these successful fundraising events, the daily struggle to keep the building and the reading room going proved to be too much for the WCTU. By 1890, Santa Monica had been an incorporated city for four years and the population had reached 1580. The WCTU proposed turning the library of 800 volumes over to the city of Santa Monica. The proposal reads as follows:

Award winning floral display which helped fund the reading room in 1888.

It appearing to the members of this society that said society is unable to pay the current expenses of the library belonging to them, and believing it will be for its best interest to donate the said library to the town of Santa Monica, a municipal organization duly incorporated and existing under the laws of this state, to be carried on by the said town in accordance with the laws of this state regulating public libraries, it is therefor

Resolved that this society does hereby give, donate and bequeath to said town of Santa Monica all its said library, together with all appurtenances belonging thereto, for the purpose of maintaining a public library in connection with a free reading room.*

It was signed and dated November 14, 1890. The town trustees accepted the gift and appointed the first library trustees and the first city librarian. Miss Elfie Mosse, granddaughter of Mrs. Asenath Larimer who had been instru-

*Luther Ingersoll, *Ingersoll's Century History, Santa Monica Bay Cities* (Los Angeles, 1908) p. 273.

mental in the subscription drive for the reading room a few years earlier, was appointed librarian in December 1890. Two rooms in the Bank of Santa Monica at Oregon Avenue (later Santa Monica Blvd.) and Third Street were set aside for the library.

The first report of the library after it was turned over to the city reads "Report of Santa Monica Public Library, commencing December 5th. The book list names 808 books; the records show fifteen books that have been out for several months. The list of subscribers during the month is twenty-eight—sixteen of them new on the list. Receipts for month, $7.25. Donation of a year's subscription of the following magazines: *Scribner's, Popular Science Monthly, The Forum, Harper's Monthly, Puck and Judge.*"

Even with the required fee of 25 cents a month to borrow books the library was still in need of funds. However, in

Bank of Santa Monica, the first location of the Santa Monica Library in 1890.

March 1893 the library was made free to the public. By then, the library had 1,800 volumes and by 1898 had expanded to include another room. In March 1903, the library moved to the new City Hall located at Fourth and Oregon Avenue which provided more room, but was not meant to be a permanent location.

As the city of Santa Monica grew, so did the library collection. Members of the public wanted a library building of their own and thought that it might be possible to secure funding from Andrew Carnegie as so many other towns were doing. Early in 1903, Mrs. J.H. Clark wrote to Mr. Carnegie making a plea for a library building in Santa Monica. His reply in April reads as follows:

> Madam: Responding to your communication on behalf of Santa Monica. If the city agree by resolution of Councils to maintain a Free Public Library at cost of not less than Twelve Hundred and Fifty Dollars a year, and provide a suitable site for the building, Mr. Carnegie will be pleased to furnish Twelve Thousand Five Hundred Dollars to erect a Free Public Library Building for Santa Monica.*

Since the city was already spending more than the requisite amount to support the library annually, the only thing needed was a site. Within a short time, the citizens raised $3,982.50 and purchased a lot on the northeast corner of Oregon Avenue (later Santa Monica Blvd.) and Fifth Street. Work began on the building in January 1904 and it opened to the public on August 11 of the same year.

Written rules from the early days of the library make interesting reading. By 1906, the reading room was open every day, including Sunday, although no books could be borrowed on Sundays and holidays. Membership was open to residents of Santa Monica and to non-residents who owned real estate in the city, but could be obtained only by

*Ibid., p. 275.

Carnegie library building built in 1904.

providing references or security in "order to eliminate such patrons who by reason of death, removal from town, or other causes can neither draw books themselves nor secure against the loss from the negligence of others." Another rule states "The library is in communication with the City Health Officer and in the event of contagious or infectious disease existing in the household of a book borrower, such borrower shall be immediately notified to turn over such library books as he may have to the Health Officer for disinfection." In those days, books could be borrowed for a maximum of fourteen days, and magazines for seven days. Borrowers were limited to two books, one being non-fiction. Overdue fines were two cents a day.*

The Library's 1912-13 annual report indicates the collection had grown to 18,568 volumes. Circulation totaled 80,666. Expenditures for the year included $2445.87 for books, $46.25 for fumigating and exterminating bats, and $2.60 for chopping wood and kindling. The collection was already beginning to outgrow the building and the City

*Rules of the Santa Monica Public Library, 1906.

Librarian added in the report "If Mr. Carnegie is not favorable to an additional sum for the enlargement of the building, we think a request should be made from the citizens through a bond issue. The library could and should be made a social center, and without additional land the plant could be improved to meet many conditions along this line. As Santa Monica has not a Y.M.C.A. or rest room for men or women, every one interested could help to make the library a general center for all." At this time the number of books that could be borrowed was increased to four, of which only two could be fiction.

The Library continued to grow but it was another fourteen years before the building was enlarged. In 1926, a bond issue was passed by the voters in the sum of $50,000 for reconstruction and expansion of the library on the same site. The small Carnegie structure was enlarged and remodeled into a Spanish-style design by E.J. Baume. Two wings were added on either side; the West wing included a combined art gallery and lecture room, and the East wing became a reading room for newspapers and periodicals. It

Enlarged library as it appeared in 1927.

opened to the public on November 18, 1927. Part of the reopening ceremonies included the presentation of a check to Miss Mosse, the City Librarian, "with the idea that she shall take a vacation trip to Honolulu." The mayor assured the crowd of supporters that she would be given the time off whenever she wished, but is is not known if she took the trip.

A memorable feature of the remodeled library was the art that covered its interior walls. Artist Stanton Macdonald-Wright was commissioned to paint murals for the adult section by the Public Works Administration Project. His theme depicted man's struggle with nature, both real and imaginary. The 2,000-square-foot composition was painted on detachable plywood panels so that the work of art could be removed and preserved if the building did not endure.

Macdonald-Wright began the project, which took 18 months, in February 1934. Although he was assisted by two technicians the actual painting was entirely his work. The

Lobby showing the Macdonald-Wright murals depicting the technical and imaginative pursuits of primitive man.

Close-up of one of the Macdonald-Wright murals with the artist.

resulting murals made a lasting and powerful impression on library users and also enjoyed considerable critical success.

In the children's section, called the Boys and Girls Room, Eulalie Wilson, an illustrator of children's books, painted the murals. Peter Pan, Cinderella, Goldilocks and other characters peeked over bookcases and around pillars. Twenty-five years after painting the originals, Eulalie, as

Murals in the Boys and Girls Room depict characters from children's books.

Close-up of Peter Pan from the children's murals by Eulalie.

Eulalie touches up the murals 25 years after they were first painted.

she liked to be known, returned and was dismayed to see that the murals were showing their age. She offered to paint new murals, but the existing work was so beloved that she was asked to do only a touch up job. When the public saw her working, they were afraid the murals were being replaced and many tearful or angry calls were made to the library.

As the city continued to grow, the library became more crowded. The community realized that larger quarters were needed and that the unreinforced masonry building was structurally unsafe. In addition, it was a fire hazard due to unsafe wiring. In the 1950's and early 1960's, a community group of citizens began to publicize the need for a larger library facility. In 1962, a bond issue was passed by the voters and land was purchased on the corner of Sixth Street and Santa Monica Blvd. Construction of a new library began in February 1964 and opened to the public in September 1965. Since the new building was only one block away from the old, boxes of books were transported by conveyor belt instead of moving trucks. Teams of staff and volunteers loaded and unloaded the books. Staff members remember that the move also took place during a September heat wave and that the new building was not air conditioned at the time.

Unfortunately, the new library did not include a place for the Macdonald-Wright murals even though they were removable, and they were temporarily stored in the basement. Later the murals were accepted by the Smithsonian Institution. One of the panels is now on display at the Santa Monica Airport. The murals by Eulalie were painted directly on the walls of the old library and could not be moved. The old building was sold to Century Federal Savings and Loan Association and was demolished in 1974 in spite of two groups of local citizens who tried to block the demolition.

Exterior of the new Main Library built in 1965.

Interior of new Main Library showing spacious reading area and skylights.

During the next few years the library flourished, supported by an appreciative citizenry. But in the late 1970's the mood of California voters changed and Proposition 13, a measure to limit property taxes, was passed. The result was decreased support for municipal services in Santa Monica, as throughout the state. Although the library was not the target of disaffected taxpayers, it suffered along with other city departments. Hours of service were curtailed in the branches and Main Library, and staff was reduced. However, supporters of the library quickly rallied to lobby the City Council and most of the Proposition 13 cuts affecting the library were rescinded in a short time.

The Main Library suffered another crisis when asbestos was discovered in the composition of its acoustic ceiling. In 1983 the ceiling was disturbed by an attempt to clean heavily soiled areas, beginning a three-year period of controversy about the fate of the building. Removal of the asbestos was estimated at $2,000,000. Since it was becoming increasingly obvious that the building would soon be too small for its growing collections and services, city management proposed building another Main Library on a new site as a possible solution. A space and site study was done and two public hearings were held, in which library users made clear their opposition to any change of location. Library staff also opposed a new site, not wishing to remain in a building they considered dangerous while a new library was constructed. Finally, a decision was made to close the Main Library for asbestos abatement and the doors closed in August 1986. The majority of the collection was put in storage, and staff was relocated to the Santa Monica airport and the three branches.

The building was reopened in March 1988 with some minor changes in layout. The biggest change was a new automated circulation system and catalog. For five weeks

During closure for asbestos removal, the building was stripped bare.

prior to opening, the library staff and volunteers spent many hours matching all the books and other materials in the collection with barcodes. The new computer not only made checking the books in and out much easier and faster, but also enabled staff and patrons to find out exactly how many copies were in the libraries and in which branches they were located. For several months the new computer lived side by side with the old card catalog but in January 1989, the card catalog was removed completely. Another advantage of the new technology was that patrons who had home computers could "dial-in" to the library catalog from home.

Even before the closing it was obvious that with the steadily increasing usage the Main Library had once again outgrown its building. Since the opening 25 years earlier, the adult book collection had increased by 75%, the children's collection by 50% and other collections such as periodicals and audio-visual materials were growing at astonishing rates.

Card catalog in the old library building.

Drawers of cards have been replaced by SAM, an automated catalog.

In 1988 H. Richard Horst, president of the Friends of the Santa Monica Public Library and a former Library Board chairperson, headed a committee backing a bond measure to purchase land adjacent to the building for future expansion. The bond issue was approved by voters in November 1988. As the library begins its second century, plans are being made for expanding the building to accommodate new services and collections.

In its Centennial Year the library can look back on its

progress from one room with one librarian to becoming the largest public library on the Westside of Los Angeles. It will continue to grow to meet the informational and recreational needs of the public. Whatever the future holds in the way of new technology, the Santa Monica Public Library will continue to serve the citizens as it always has.

Ocean Park Branch, an original Carnegie building.

CHAPTER 2

The Branches

THE OCEAN PARK BRANCH

The south side of Santa Monica, known as Ocean Park, developed quickly into a seaside amusement center. Piers, bathhouses, a golf course and race track, all made this a popular spot for residents and vacationers alike. By 1905 the boundaries of the city had extended to include an area from Eighth Street and Marine in the south to Twenty-seventh Street and Montana in the north.

As the city grew, the need for branch libraries became evident. As early as 1906, there was a book exchange in the Ocean Park area located in the Clapp Brother's Drug Store on Pier Avenue. Borrowers could return library books to this location on Tuesdays and Fridays and send in an order for additional books to be picked up at a later date. However, it did not meet the demand for a full service library. A committee was appointed to select possible sites for a branch library in the Ocean Park area with consideration being given to accessibility, sightliness and price. A lot on the northeast corner of Ocean Park Blvd. and Main Street was purchased for $8,000 and the mayor wrote to the Carnegie Corporation requesting a grant to help build the building. The request for $12,500 was granted; the Ocean Park Branch opened to the public on February 15, 1918.

At the beginning of World War II, the branch's basement meeting room was used by the USO until it moved to larger quarters downtown. On April 4, 1945, the room was converted to a Young People's Room. Teenagers gathered here for study and games. Popular magazines and books were kept here but they were not part of the regular library collection. A radio played constantly, and the room was staffed by a social worker rather than a librarian. When the Jewish Community Center opened nearby in October 1949, the teenagers moved there. The basement room was then devoted to the children's books since they had been housed in very cramped quarters on the main floor. This was staffed by a children's librarian but was only open during the day. In 1959 the children's books were moved back to the main floor so that they would be available all hours the branch was open. The basement room was used for library programs, films and community meetings.

By the mid-1970's, it was apparent that the original

Young People's Room in the basement of the Ocean Park Branch was a popular gathering place for teenagers in 1945.

American Heritage Discussion Group, 1953-54, met in the basement room of the Ocean Park Branch.

branch building was inadequate. It was built of unreinforced masonry, it was too small for the needs of the community it served, and it was not accessible to the handicapped. In 1976, a feasibility study and public hearings were conducted to explore building a new branch, but it was made clear that the community wanted to keep the familiar building. It was declared an official city landmark in May 1977.

A plan to expand and remodel the building without changing the "Carnegie" look was approved and the branch closed for renovation in June 1984. Moldings and ceiling tiles were designed to complement the period look of the building. Friends of the Library raised $6,500 for new furnishings. When the Ocean Park Branch reopened in September 1985 it had a new entrance, an enlarged children's area and a community meeting room in the basement with projection booth and kitchen. The Ocean Park community

Exterior of the remodeled Ocean Park Branch looks the same, but it has been enlarged and the entrance has been moved to the side.

showed its pleasure in the "new" library by increasing usage 40%.

THE FAIRVIEW BRANCH

By 1930, Santa Monica had grown to include an area from the ocean on the west to Centinela on the east, and from Marine Street on the south to Santa Monica Canyon on the north. The city was home to over 37,000 and was proud to boast that it had a hospital, junior college and the new Douglas Aircraft Company and Clover Air Field.

The expansion of the city to the east created the need for an additional library branch. The Fairview Heights Branch opened to meet this need on July 1, 1931. The tiny storefront branch was a mere 15 feet wide, sandwiched between a small grocery store and a barber shop. It was located at 1903 20th Street, a few blocks from the present site, and was open from 2:00 pm to 6:00 pm three days a week. Some

800 books lined its walls. For relaxation, one could clamber up to the rear mezzanine and browse through the limited reference and magazine materials.

City Librarian Elfie Mosse inaugurated the facility, which had been originally named the Irwin Heights Branch. After most of the books had been stamped with this name, it was changed to the Fairview Heights Branch. All the books had to be re-stamped! Nellie "Dollie" Sullivan was appointed Branch Librarian and served continuously in this capacity as the branch grew and changed locations until her retirement in September 1965.

By 1942, the storefront library could no longer handle its increased patronage and there was a need to move the library closer to two schools in the area. Katherine Whelan was City Librarian at this time and she headed the effort to relocate the branch. L.J. Shimmer offered to erect the new

Members of the summer reading club gather outside the first location of the Fairview Heights Branch, c. 1940.

Second location of Fairview Branch at 2030 Pico Blvd.

building, suitable for a library and rent it to the city. The new facility at 2030 Pico Blvd. opened its doors to the public on July 13, 1942, with the name shortened to Fairview Branch Library. Six years later, the city of Santa Monica bought the property.

During World War II staff and patrons vividly remember seeing the bulging barrage balloons and the camouflage of the nearby Douglas Aircraft factory. As families came to work at Douglas, use of the branch increased. Some of the parents worked long shifts and the children often spent many hours at the library after school.

During this time, Branch Librarian Nellie Sullivan initiated a unique service by holding one of the first preschool story times on the West Coast. She had read about such story times in libraries in the East and wanted to start one at her own library. It was so successful that similar story times soon began at the Main Library and other branches.

By the year 1952, the Fairview Branch boasted a circulation of over 35,000 books, and 3000 registered borrowers. It became obvious that the facility could no longer handle the increasing burden. City Librarian Hilda Glaser was responsible for constructing the present Fairview Branch at 2101 Ocean Park Blvd. in 1956. The floor space of over 5000 square feet was ample for the collection that numbered 20,000 volumes at that time. Circulation was about 100,000 per year. Readers could relax in the landscaped patio areas, one for the adults and the other for children. It provided a pleasant atmosphere for conducting children's story hours and summer reading programs.

In 1978, City Librarian Carol Aronoff found the opportunity to expand the Fairview Branch by obtaining a Federal grant. Before the end of the year, a new community meeting room seating 75 and accessible to the handicapped was added, along with an alcove for periodicals and staff office space. During the time the Main Library was closed for asbestos removal, the meeting room was used for a Reference Center. Reference librarians and reference books were

Interior of the new Fairview Branch, showing the ample floor space.

available to the public and telephone reference service was provided from this location.

By 1989, the Fairview Branch Library had an annual circulation of about 140,000 and 37,000 books filled its shelves. There were over 100 magazines and newspapers plus records, cassettes, and a significant collection of Spanish language materials serving a large Latino community in the Pico Blvd. area.

MONTANA AVENUE BRANCH

The Montana Avenue Branch began life as a storefront library on Lincoln's birthday 1952. Just as the two branches on the south side of Santa Monica had been opened in response to the need for service closer to the neighborhoods, the north side of the city was in need of library service for its community. The branch was located in a rented building at 1528-30 Montana Avenue. Two large gifts of books, the Lewis Browne collection and the Samuel McClure collection were used in part for the new library's holdings. In addition, according to the Santa Monica *Evening Outlook,* many children's books were donated "from homes in which sons and daughters have outgrown juvenile books." New books were also purchased to form an original collection of 4,292 books. The new branch thrived, and by 1958, under the direction of Branch Librarian Mrs. Eleanor Higgins, the circulation totaled 80,325 items.

After seven years the branch had outgrown its rented quarters and plans were underway for a new building. Preliminary plans were approved in January 1959. After lengthy negotiations, two lots on Montana Avenue were purchased, one for $36,850 and the other for $35,200. Groundbreaking ceremonies for the new building at 1704 Montana Avenue were conducted on August 20, 1959 and the library opened to the public on March 1, 1960. The library building

Original location of the Montana Avenue Branch, 1952.

Interior of Montana Avenue Branch on opening day, 1952.

Elfie Mosse, City Librarian
1890-1939

Katherine Whelan, City Librarian 1939-1951.

CHAPTER 3

The City Librarians

A library is more than buildings and books. Many departments and individuals work together to create the organization. Although the Santa Monica Public Library began as a small collection managed by a single person, it soon grew to reflect the size and diversity of the burgeoning community of Santa Monica.

The first librarian appointed by the City, Miss Elfie Mosse was the entire library staff for the first fourteen years. One day, in the rooms over the bank, Roy Jones, a library trustee, found her washing windows. He saw to it that a janitor was hired immediately and may have paid the janitor's salary out of his own pocket. Another of the early trustees had a running battle with Miss Mosse because of his firm belief that books should be arranged on the shelf by color rather than subject. Although she conceded that it might be aesthetically more pleasing to adhere to a color scheme, she insisted on following a subject classification. Throughout her 49 years as librarian, Elfie Mosse believed in the right of the public to seek knowledge without the hindrance of censorship or prejudice against any class, sect or part of society.

Miss Mosse later had additional help during summers when the library was busier, but no permanent staff was added until Miss Grace Baxter was hired. A second staff member, Katherine Whelan, was added in 1907. She was appointed assistant librarian in 1920 and upon the retirement of Miss Mosse, was appointed City Librarian on July 1, 1939. Miss Whelan was the Librarian responsible for enlarging the staff, developing the branch libraries and creating many of the library departments that exist today. She retired in 1951 after 44 years of service. She is remembered by staff who worked with her as a feisty woman with an Irish temper who demanded the best of herself and her staff.

In 1951 when Miss Whelan retired, Mr. Harold Helmrich was selected as City Librarian. He came to Santa Monica from Yakima, Washington, but held the post only from September 1951 until February 1952. While a search was being held for a new librarian, Mrs. Susan Horn from the Reference Department was Acting Librarian.

The search for a new librarian ended with the selection of Miss Hilda Glaser who came to the city from St. Petersburg,

Hilda Glaser, City Librarian 1952-1972

Florida. For the next 20 years, she headed the library. She began planning for a new Main Library building in the late 50's, and by 1961 she had organized a support group, the Friends of the Santa Monica Public Library, to promote and raise funds for the new building which opened in 1965. It was under her direction that the Montana Avenue Branch was opened and later she oversaw construction of the present branch. The Fairview Branch also moved to its present location in a new building constructed during her tenure. Miss Glaser was the guiding force that brought Santa Monica into the Metropolitan Cooperative Library System in 1968, giving residents access to the resources of 20 libraries in the Los Angeles area. During this period the annual book circulation nearly doubled to over one million. Miss Glaser retired in November 1972.

Her successor was Mrs. Patricia Terrill Brownell who headed the Reference Department for many years and had been the Assistant City Librarian. She retired after two

Patricia Terrill Brownell, City
Librarian 1972-1974.

years as City Librarian. In the short time she was the Librarian, the library continued its growth and by the time of her retirement, the annual circulation was over 1.1 million.

In 1974, the new City Librarian was a young woman who had worked in a number of departments in the library. Miss Carol Armstrong, later Carol Aronoff, had worked in the Reference, Audiovisual and Circulation Departments in the six years she had been employed in the library prior to being named City Librarian. During her tenure, the Ocean Park Branch was enlarged and remodeled, the Fairview Branch was enlarged, the Main Library was closed for 19 months for removal of asbestos and remodeling, and plans for future expansion of the library were begun. Under her direction the records of library holdings were converted from catalog cards to machine-readable form and an online computer

Carol Armstrong Aronoff,
City Librarian 1974-1989.

catalog and circulation system were installed. The literacy program for adult learners was another service innovation under Mrs. Aronoff. She was active in professional activities and served as president of the California Library Association in 1982. In September 1989, she resigned. Ms. Molly Richardson, Assistant City Librarian, was appointed Acting Librarian while the search for a new director took place.

Early in 1990, the search for a new City Librarian culminated when Ms. Winona Allard was appointed. She came to Santa Monica after working for Los Angeles County Library for the past 12 years. Her previous experience included work in adult services and reference and language learning centers, and her education included degrees from UCLA, the University of Michigan and Harvard. Her tasks will include planning for future library expansion.

Winona Allard,
City Librarian 1990-.

The Boys and Girls Room had its own entrance in the original
Carnegie Main Library.

CHAPTER 4

Services and Staff

CHILDREN'S SERVICES

From the time of the first Carnegie building, the library has had a special room for children. Miss Mosse's first assistant, Miss Grace Baxter, initiated a student's class, selecting books to meet the demand for help with school work. In 1930, the first librarian who specialized in children's work was hired. Mrs. Mercer Watson Lucas created a summer reading course in the children's department each year and promoted children's literature for 15 years. In addition, authors of children's books often spoke at the library. Throughout the years, local authors such as Margaret Leighton, Monica Shannon and Scott O'Dell have enchanted groups of children at library programs. One of the most popular visitors was not an author but a dog! Lassie was brought to the library by trainer Rudd Weatherwax after a biography of the movie collie had been written by local author John H. Rothwell.

Mrs. Lucas was succeeded in 1945 by Miss Mary Margaret Dyer who guided children's services for the next 25 years. Following the successful preschool story time launched at the Fairview Branch earlier, in 1946 Miss Dyer began a regular series of story times. During her years of service, the library was known for the popular storytimes presented

Mrs. Mercer Watson Lucas supervising
a children's program, c. 1930.

Children's author Margaret Leighton autographs books for her
young fans.

Storytime with Miss Mary Margaret Dyer was popular with children of all ages.

The Library Players, c. 1954.

to both preschoolers and older children. Summer programs were well patronized also. One unusual summer event was a "bookmobile," a pickup truck that carried books and librarians to the parks and to the children there. Also during this period, the Boys and Girls Room sponsored the Library Players, a group of local children who put on plays in the library.

Successors to Miss Dyer, Mrs. Virginia McShane and Mrs. Ami Kirby have built upon the framework provided by these pioneers and have continued to encourage a love of reading in all the children who come into the library. Programs for children have included puppet shows, films, story times, craft programs, and visits by authors.

ADULT SERVICES

As the adult collection grew in size and complexity, residents needed more assistance in using the library, and reference service became an important part of the overall service. At first librarians helped users choose and find books in the local collection. Then they provided answers from library reference books to those in need of information. Later they were able to locate materials anywhere in the United States and Canada and produce them via interlibrary loan. Today they are able to research complex questions through a sophisticated network of information and referral sources, both inside and outside of the library . . . and still provide the basic service of helping users find the books they want.

The Reference Department evolved into Adult Services and now encompasses Reference, Periodicals, Collection Development, Interlibrary Loan and Santa Monica Reads, the literacy program. It oversees outreach programs to special segments of the Santa Monica population: young adults, the homebound, and the Spanish-speaking community. In 1973, Hilda Glaser, after retiring as City Librarian, began the volunteer Service to Shut-Ins which brings books and other materials to those unable to come to the library. Outreach to the Latino community began in 1978 based upon recommendations of a library taskforce researching the needs of Spanish-speaking residents. The literacy program, begun in 1988 with a grant from the California State Library, provides tutors for adults who wish to improve their reading and writing skills.

Collection development activities also expanded as the needs of the community grew. In 1896, six years after the founding of the city library, there were 19,265 books, 29 magazine subscriptions, and 11 newspapers. By 1989 the collection had grown to 324,119 books, 898 magazine subscriptions, and 84 newspapers. Materials in new formats were added as they became available. In 1961 the first periodicals on microfilm were added. By 1989 the library held over 5,000 microfilm and 14,000 microfiche units. A fascinating collection of 2,500 historical photographs of Santa Monica and Venice has been developed, and government documents, pamphlets and maps have been added over the years.

Behind the scenes in the Technical Services Department all the books and other materials are ordered, cataloged and processed. In the early days of the library, each book was numbered and recorded by hand in a large accession book. Although cataloging is now done by computer, there is still much manual work that has to be done. The books have to be identified with a library stamp, covered with plastic to protect the dust jacket, and provided with a date due slip or pocket.

In 1947 the Santa Monica Public Library inaugurated the first public library Film Department in California. It began with three 16mm films and projection equipment and rapidly expanded. Over the next eight months, the collection grew to 22 films, several of which were deposited in the library by business firms. Soon, regular film programs in the Main Library and branches were being presented.

The service was expanded to include recordings in 1949,

The Films and Recordings Department, a first in California.

when a public appeal for phonograph records brought almost 200 donations. By 1951 the fledgling department, called Films and Recordings, had outgrown its space and in 1953 a new area partitioned off from the reading rooms was created.

In 1965, when the new Main Library was opened, the Films and Recordings Department was included as an important service point on the ground floor. By the time the building was remodeled in 1986, the department, now called Audiovisual Services, needed even more space and was moved to the second floor. The collection included not only films and records, but audiocassettes, videocassettes, and compact discs and books-on-cassette. Braille Institute recordings and players for the visually handicapped are also part of the service.

The annual Boyle-Hutchinson award, given by the California Library Association for excellence in audiovisual librarianship, is named in part for the first Santa Monica film librarian, Miss Gene Hutchinson, in recognition of her influential role in promoting audiovisual services in California libraries.

Gene Hutchinson, a pioneer film librarian.

MEMORIES OF STAFF AND FRIENDS

A number of librarians have continued to work in the library for many years, especially in the Reference Dept. Mrs. Amy Webb brought a lifetime of reading to her work in the Reference Department and worked there from 1923 to 1948. Susan Horn worked for the library many years and was Acting City Librarian at one time while a new City Librarian was being sought. In addition it has not been unusual for staff members to begin their career in the library as a page, or shelver, and work their way up the career ladder. A number of librarians both past and present have been pages, clerks and then gone on to get a professional library degree. One librarian still vividly remembers working as a page one summer and erasing pencil marks in books, one by one. When they were needed to fetch newspapers or periodicals, the clerk summoned them by clicking a metal "cricket." She still jumps when she hears that click!

In addition to staff members who spent many years in the library, there have been family dynasties in the Santa Monica Library. One family has contributed four staff members throughout the years, both as paraprofessionals and as librarians. Fairview Branch Librarian Nellie Pierson Sullivan was joined by her sister Elva Pierson Hoeger, who worked as a clerk and then as a library assistant from 1945-54. Both of Elva Hoeger's daughters became librarians and worked for the library also. Ami Hoeger Kirby is currently the Head of Children's Services. Her sister Gretchen Hoeger Hollingsworth worked as a catalog librarian from 1985-87 before going on to other libraries. Other families have had siblings working in different library departments as pages, or children or grandchildren of staff members working in various branches or departments.

The library even has non-human staff! One of the most recognized staff members currently is Woody, a ventriliquist's dummy who has "lived" at the Ocean Park Branch and the Fairview Branch Library. Woody works with Ms. Ilene Cohen, a children's librarian and has his own library card.

In addition, the libraries have had regular furred and feathered friends. In 1954, a staff newsletter indicated that the majority of library employees owned cats. While there has never been an official library cat, several branches have had neighbor cats that tried to move in. One cat at Fairview liked sitting on the open unabridged dictionary. At Montana Branch, a local cat kept returning no matter how many times it was ejected. Patrons have wanted to bring their pets into the library also and have sometimes succeeded despite rules to the contrary. One woman kept her small dog in a basket and brought it into the library. One of the most unusual visitors was brought in by a woman who wanted to see some books about birds. She was still uncertain if the bird in the illustration was the variety she wanted, so she pulled the cloth off the bundle she was carrying and the bird she was carrying in a cage began to cheep. She had raised the bird from a chick which had fallen out of a nest, and now she knew that it was a housefinch.

The original Board of Trustees appointed when the library was incorporated into the City of Santa Monica became a chartered entity, known as the Library Board, with the adoption of the City Charter in 1947. The mission statement was, "The Santa Monica Public Library Board shall have charge of the administration of the Santa Monica Public Library." The charter provisions state that the board shall have powers and be required to make and enforce by-laws, rules and regulations as may be necessary for the administration, government and protection of the library; approve or disapprove the appointment of a Librarian; and accept money, personal property or real estate donated to the library or its predecessor.

One of the first trustees was Abbot Kinney, builder of the nearby Venice canals. The board has attracted other service-minded citizens who have served many years including Dr. David J. Donnan, Robert Nittinger, Estelle Seiger and H. Richard Horst.

Another group lending the library its support is the Friends of the Santa Monica Library. From their inception in 1961 to advance the citizens' campaign to build a new

Main Library they have provided for special programs, donated furniture and equipment, and supported the Service to Shut-Ins with funds and volunteers. Through sales of donated and used library books, plus other fundraising events, they have provided funds to refurbish the Main Library Auditorium, to help purchase a grand piano for musical programs and to partly furnish the Ocean Park Branch when it was remodeled.

Throughout the years, the Santa Monica Public Library has attracted many users from all over the Southern California area, including many writers. Past librarians remember authors like Christopher Isherwood, Lewis Browne, Thomas Mann, Margaret Leighton, Sid Fleishman, Kin Platt, and John Dean who used the library for their research or their work. In November 1946, the library hosted an author's reception for authors living in the Santa Monica

Local authors wait their turn at the Author's Reception, 1946.
Left to right: Jean Leslie Cornett, Craig Rice, Lawrence Lipton, Margaret Leighton and Earle Schenk.

area. Mystery author Craig Rice, Leon Feuchwanger, Margaret Leighton and others appeared. Since the Santa Monica area is home to many actors and actresses, it is not unusual to see a famous face buried in a book. Library buildings have been used in movies and television scenes too, although usually as something other than a library!

Over the past 100 years, the library has seen many changes. From a collection of 800 books in a small room over a bank, the collection has grown to approximately 400,000 items housed in four library buildings. In addition to books, magazines and newspapers, the collections include government documents, historic slides and photos, phonograph records, audiocassettes, videocassettes, compact discs, 16mm films, pamphlets and maps. While it is not known what kinds of materials will be added as new technology evolves, it is certain that the Santa Monica Public Library will continue to provide information and recreational materials for the public they serve. As the staff looks forward to the second hundred years of the library service, plans are being made to expand again. While details are not yet worked out, the citizens of Santa Monica will continue to find the library an integral part of their lives. One hundred years ago, when the fledgling library was handed over to the city, no one dreamed that the library would grow to include so many diverse formats and technologies. In another hundred years, the library may change greatly, but it will still remain relevant and vital. The tradition of service that extends from Elfie Mosse to the present will not be broken.

LOCATIONS OF MAIN LIBRARY BUILDING

Date	Building	Location
1884-1888	McKinnie's Drug Store	3rd Street
1888-1890	WCTU Building	3rd Street
1890-1903	Bank of Santa Monica	3rd Street and Oregon (Santa Monica Bl.)
1903-1904	City Hall	4th Street and Oregon (Santa Monica Bl.)
1904-1926	Carnegie Building	5th Street and Santa Monica Blvd.
1926-1965	Enlarged Carnegie Building	5th Street and Santa Monica Blvd.
1965-present	New building	6th Street and Santa Monica Blvd.

LOCATIONS OF BRANCH LIBRARIES

OCEAN PARK BRANCH

1918-present	Carnegie Building	Main Street and Ocean Park Blvd.

FAIRVIEW BRANCH

1931-1942	Storefront	20th Street and Delaware
1942-1956	Rented building	20th Street and Pico Blvd.
1956-present	Current building	21st Street and Ocean Park Blvd.

MONTANA AVENUE BRANCH

1952-1960	Storefront	15th Street and Montana Ave.
1960-present	Current building	17th Street and Montana Ave.

Index